HOLDING
UNFAILING

For Neil,

Hoping you will enjoy
this, my second volume.

EDWARD RAGG

E.R.

INDEPENDENT INNOVATIVE INTERNATIONAL

Published by Cinnamon Press
Meirion House
Tanygrisiau
Blaenau Ffestiniog
Gwynedd, LL41 3SU
www.cinnamonpress.com

The right of Edward Ragg to be identified as author of this work has been asserted by him in accordance with the Copyright, Designs and Patent Act, 1988. Copyright © 2017 Edward Ragg
ISBN: 978-1-910836-51-4

British Library Cataloguing in Publication Data. A CIP record for this book can be obtained from the British Library.

Designed and typeset in Palatino by Cinnamon Press. Printed in Poland.

Cover design by Adam Craig from original artwork, 'Guang Hua Road' by Alex Dougherty, used with kind permission, © Alex Dougherty.

Cinnamon Press is represented in the UK by Inpress Ltd and in Wales by the Welsh Books Council.

Acknowledgements

I am grateful to the following publications in which some of these poems first appeared, sometimes in earlier versions: *BODY, Cha: An Asian Literary Journal, Cordite Poetry Review, Envoi, Orbis, Papercuts.*

'Fragment: Unaccountable', 'Path Finding' and 'The Empress of Peonies' first appeared in English and Mandarin Chinese versions in *Enclave* (ed. Zhang Er) as part of a special feature, including poems from *A Force That Takes* (Cinnamon Press, 2013) also in English and Mandarin. 'Mutton Fat Jade' was first published online as a prize-winning poem from the *2009 Troubadour International Poetry Competition.* 'Punctuation Points' was first published online as a prize-winning poem from the *2014 Troubadour International Poetry Competition.*

Special thanks are due to Jan Fortune, Penelope Shuttle, Wang Ao, Eleanor Goodman, Chris Yates, Alex Dougherty, Eileen Lee, Nazeer Chowdhury, Bernard O'Donoghue and Sarah Howe.

A very special debt of gratitude must go to my dear wife, and ultimate companion, Fongyee Walker.

Contents

For my parents, Pudens Leonard Ragg and Josephine Ragg

...]θε θῦμον
...]μι πάμπαν
...]δύναμαι

] heart
] absolutely
] I can

Sappho, *Fragment 4*, trans. Anne Carson

Holding Unfailing

Fragment: Unaccountable

I lean towards
your city

but do not move
...] as China floods

past, its floods past
in the present metal.

The continual ships
of the continuous river

...] the metal of our days
to you I lean and see

today's tomorrow
yesterday

Great Southern in Crystal

Bright theatrics of karri
and the dark orange

earth of dust tracks brushed
with the carbonized stumps

of trunks caught in wildfire…

Things prepared to speak
as if they would be speaking.

Millions of years have worn
this place: elephant-hind rocks,

beaches white as Antarctica,
the air more dazzling than crystal.

And I believe nothing
may answer death

except that which lives
in the terminal places:

the Southern Ocean
flagrant in its waves.

How could they arrive
capable, gutted from

surrender and the hulls
of ships also broken?

The exterior ridges
(within us), the interiors

(without) which
the taxonomy

of rocks elaborates,
our most mineral desires…

So that we breathe
the untouchable light again.

Holding Unfailing

The unencumbered light
of the yellowish city

from whose rays
the primary colours

of awnings, poster-boards,
books are leached.

It is a light which
seems to wish

there were a world
elsewhere,

though we cling to this
and conjugate by days:

to hope, to have,
to hold, to hang onto...

Desire the putative cause,
desire of the putative cause

fathomless in the depths
of that light.

There is no surface
it may not touch...

of which it is not
capable of touching

and may bathe us
in the same regret, yet

encumbered, entrenched,
febrile, magnificent.

Path Finding

Leaving Mount Barker
in a borrowed four-by-four

along executed routes
we edged toward Margaret River.

Where tarmac yielded
to the skittering stones

of a freshly levelled stretch,
the low winter sun

flooded our retinas,
the speedometer dropping

like the sunken ocean
until, gingerly, you strained

headfirst out of the window
to look ahead…

This faith was faith as faith
because unreferred:

the unseen road,
my love for you

the same,
only the same.

Believing no less
in parable than in fact

for what seemed days
and still may

today in the years
you have guided me

and guide me
I know not where.

Sole Food

These tattered old boots still
grip the pock-marked tarmac

and have traipsed, I reflect,
the streets of Moscow,

a Queensland pineapple farm,
the dust-caked alleyways

of Beijing... to arrive
at this point where,

stumbling from memory,
I read my mother's deft

needlework stitched into
each lace-etched tongue

a name in red capitals:
mine.

Eighteen years on
my tongue is initialled

with those same hands and
inscribed with what lies now

between the knots of our reach:
the Mongolian steppes,

the Eastern lakes,
the curious cathedrals

of her origins in
needle-box Swiss chalets.

So if I am ever lost,
she may nominate

my unspoken state,
hauling unspeakable loads

across the broken curbs
of a foreign city.

Wang Ao and the Lobster

Wang Ao, poet and translator, born Qingdao, sits in New Haven.
He is about to cook a ten-pound Maine lobster for his friends.

I.

This creature, Ao, swims in the ocean of your sense
and continents. Not eccentric, not de Nerval's
poor pet who plumbed 'the secrets of the deep'.

You read, stanza by stanza, a Buddhist tract
and then, with reverence, take the moment
by its tail, the cleaver shedding juice

like an idea of birth or ceremony, as if life
were never sweeter, no, nor more savoury.
Your friends bicker over the dipping sauce.

II.

Ambassador, you are stationed in New Haven
mouthing characters from the Tang… translated,
tongue-twitching English by return of Beijing,

or back again, my own voice stroke-marked
and unfolded like a scroll. Give thanks:
the one, the other, the lobster from its tail,

claw by claw, snapped, but not butter-dunked,
in steam-soft garlic, ginger slice, pronounced.
Our teeth are flapping crackers in the wind.

III.

Years ago, at a fishery, a plucky one, unshackled,
flicked the Rolex from a soft-shelled man
and made as if it would splash to Switzerland

to take its chances with the perch—even if watch
and lake meant death. Your lobster voyages
by the precision clock: Maine by Florida,

Key West by Panama, then the long soak
to Qingdao where, as a boy, you sucked his shell
and, now, this steaming moment, slurp again

until the moons of your fingernails are
orange-warm pink. Later, in clutch of books,
his prized pincers bask in the New Haven sun.

It reminds you of your prehensile state,
all baby-snappers and drooling; of what, even here,
in the shell of the place, you would grasp again.

The Road of Excess

This grey morning
in which the cityscape

swirls with winter smoke
dense for all it clouds...

The effective earth
and the affective mind:

all the unelaborate sides
pressing against

what grace notes
happiness may extend

to the emitting towers
and edges of things.

And the devices
at my hands:

too various to enumerate,
too complex to comprehend,

too absorbing to be discounted,
too distracting to be ignored,

too here to lie unsifted,
too there to be observed,

too infinite to be forsaken,
too established to be heard.

From Our Own Correspondent

From winter smoke
and the cracked earth

of the peasant fields
toiling…

to the highwayed
apartments of cities

of unimaginable complexity,
where light-skinned city folk

brush obliviously
past dark-skinned arrivals

from those same
cracked fields

disembarking at
bewildering terminals.

A new dance writes
its marks upon

the kaleidoscopic lights
of midnight floors

where youth moves
on bubbles and adrenalin.

The sleek high-speed train
touches 300 kilometres per hour

rushing obliviously
past channels of lore and algae.

That we may each move
upon the earth and leave

such marks with ease
and be forgotten.

Punctuation Points

The Comma

A stepping stone,
in the pond of meaning.

The Full-Stop

The smallest and largest
point in the universe.

The Colon

A pair of identical twins:
balancing.

The Semi-Colon

A comma;
with a chaperone.

The Hyphen

One of many bridges
across-the-pond...

The Dash

A hyphen on holiday —

Inverted Quotation Marks

'Side-burns at the
face of language'.

The Exclamation Mark

Surely this could not
happen to a full stop!

The Question Mark

But can this key, as you say,
truly unlock the world?

Guang Hua Road

Straight are the lines
along Guang Hua Lu,

lines of purposeful intent:
the CCTV tower's

cross-hatched rubik's gleam
to the right, the impregnable

fortress of Guo Mao rising
from its third if not final phase.

Over the fence, diggers
unbury the strata of Chinese

history in piece after piece,
slicing through foundations

deep as ancestry. Luxury cars
pass and there is no memento

now of the lone noodle shop
that stood in the middle

of this block for months,
its exterior walls crumbling

as the diggers and shakers
moved in…

People speak into apps
which speak back

for we are people
of need of speech.

In the blank winter sun
calligraphic billboards

canvass their futures
in visions pixelated

out of recognition:
awakening to another world

where not one of us—not one—
stands and lives to tell.

The Human Chain

i.m. Seamus Heaney (1939-2013)

I.

Your *Human Chain* shines, warms
at the edges of things the dew-soaked
light of a Mossbawn morning

reaching across the fields. Though
less definitive, openly inviting
all dimensions, almost all claims.

From the untrapped gleam of the door
ajar from its jamb to the swallow-echoing
eaves sounding in unison above the lintel.

From the murky depths of Aeneas's
prophetic trawl through *Aeneid* Book VI
to the Derry heavens: tethers, teething,

the tug and lift of birth, fate and death,
the acute interims of life, love, family.
From the Trinity of local lore to those

pathetic embraces three times attempted,
three times frustrated in a green valley
somewhere between Lethe and the Elysian fields.

All familiar and unfamiliar as your father's
last days and your son's snatch-raid
about his withering neck, the hero of the hour.

II.

And warms still, even as, book after book,
you held to, turning over in your hands
victims enshrined in peat and the divisive

chains of tribes grown familiar, unfamiliar:
each its own perpetual, internecine embrace.
Letting none forget we are bound to that desire,

that we are not bound… other than as cells
dividing like frogspawn, our destinies
not perhaps writ in some preordained tome

whatever the chain-linked fences of history.
As if, quietly, in the sodden fields of a
fading afternoon you might have stopped

short and briefly defined the air.
As if to say: once we lived here
and soon enough will be gone.

A man who used to notice such things…
No one's voice tolled more physically
in those lilting, Herculean cadences

than yours. Antaen guttural polished
in the moulds of the only heaven worth
winning perhaps: earth and its dug-out worlds.

You who knew Yeats's gaffer before
Yeats himself, because you had heard him
in the yard, catching a breath between

heaving sacks. Glanced through Kavanagh's
hedgerows or the slats of an innocent fence
or at the heavy yodeling of cattle sales,

those cries that set the metal bars
of the pens ringing and seemed to cut
the very earth in sods: the mastersingers.

III.

For you there are no minor epitaphs,
though you preferred the soft, pacific
speech of last words: *Noli timere.*

Votive breaths petering out last hopes...
which was how I found you, hearing
the news at last, walking among shades

of media, your dependable figure
cutting even here the sulphuric
bonds of Beijing's leaden air.

Not Virgil, not Dante, not even you
inhaled this unparalleled state
less reverently making the headlines.

Out of whose masks I envision you
as a boy, catching on the wireless,
chisel-toned news reports

of Allied Bombings, smoke trails
of the fire-stormed German cities
levelled or sunk into the earth.

Then, as an adolescent, around the radio
once more: clipped BBC consonants
peeling back revelations of thousands

undone in the London smog of '52,
the street-lamps and cars illuminating
no more than the density of destiny.

Eliot's city for you yet more unreal,
unhinged, yet enchained, and,
as MacNeice would warn,

the bridges down or unusable:
the only option Charon's ferry
faute de mieux, obols jangling

in his black hands when
in that mid-term break you first
contemplated the price of death.

IV.

We breathe the same air and breathe
in the language across the waters
you made and made your own singing

the disinterred marvels of a planet
lit with the precision of cut turf
like sparks from the sharpened edge

of Beowulf's steel. Each vowel seeping
from the peat-rich bog, each poem the miracle
of a sluice suddenly watering the earth.

Untitled

And so we followed
breathless but breathing

the indisputable masters:

1564-1616,
1770-1850,

1879-1955,
1908-1984...

though if we listen,
attentively, may also hear

Mary Wordsworth tugging
at young Keats's sleeve:

Mr Wordsworth is not
accustomed to being

interrupted...

Neither are we, untitled,
with no official stamp

in the fabric of our words
itching to be heard.

This was our lives.

Day of Reckoning

Philosophy teaches us
it is not possible

to become
a phenomenon

or
a sensation

and by definition
not possible

to become
an overnight sensation.

But yesterday
I saw you glimpse

yourself
in the mirror

and became
that feeling

and felt then
how by the morning

you would
be gone.

Departure

We left the Swiss Alps soaring
above the perch-green lake

and bankers' houses
and pleasure boats

criss-crossing
condensation trails...

Ten thousand terraced
vineyards turned

back on themselves.

A moment later
the pilot pointed us

to the left and to the right—
Baden and Lake Konstanz

and the Austrian Alps
beyond—with the

gentle assurance
we were Munich-bound.

I considered again
the great rape of the earth,

the zest for decimation,
then paused:

to the right and to the left
Swiss and German business folk

hugged the panes of
our sunlit commuter jet

for glimpses of
these natural wonders,

the environmental icons
of the day…

that afternoon still
receding before us.

Transfer

From terminal to terminal
of no time or the spectre

of timelessness which
illudes only at the shrine

of watch-faces glinting
in the interior white light.

People of the planet come
and do not arrive:

aspiring to the precision
mechanisms of advanced

chronometers and the same
coveted products of the same

faces of the same
personages and the same

precision mechanisms
that lie beneath all faces...

Thus I covet the unsame:
the mechanisms of

these same faces
and will not arrive.

Arrival at Santiago

'Oh, must we dream our dreams
and have them, too?'
           – Elizabeth Bishop, 'Questions of Travel'

I.

Sunrise over the Andes in lilac and pink.
A tourist's reflections, the business traveller:
each window-paned alike in the morning thaw
of appreciating things.
                    Crucial, two peoples
should share the same mountains, but each
viewed differently from the other side.
The one God, if not the same children.

In the conscious sleepwalking of the jetlagged:
here is an airport, here a gate and gangway,
here over a thousand souls inspecting
each others' passports and remarkable hand luggage
in dizzying lines of impatient immigration,
as the mountains now look down upon us
in their definitive, unfamiliar splendours.
Until we are called.

II.

Out of the hotel, somehow arrived, peeling
colonial buildings disclose an actual embassy
iron-fenced from the huddled park-bench lovers
of Santa Maria's tobogganing paths unwet.
Conscious of the gushing canal of melt-water
which insistently divides a Saturday.

On the Ave Bella Vista shop-fronts trumpet
lapis lazuli in outcrops of palms and cacti
and the mistaken red hot pokers of agave,
arranged like movie props in the balmy winter sun.
While in shadier gardens, lemons and limes dream
last-squeeze reincarnations as ceviche or Pisco Sour.

III.

At the corner, the shock—is it?—of a cross,
Don Melchor's foundation, and Virgin motionless
in the cloistral shadows. Taking an abrupt right
down Melchor Concha y Toro, so cheerful
it seems the warm yellow, mauve, and turquoise
of the houses and businesses, all shuttered and grilled.
God in the Mission doors of the same houses
and premises. God for them in the palm fronds
overhanging bundles of overhead wires and
the usual collage of unwistful bikes and cars.

IV.

Wine first brought me here and now somehow
there is an arrival of sorts, one more miracle
(having left abstraction in the higher peaks
of the imagination…).
                        Surely, Santiago, a cat
must lend her felt ears to my cupping palm?
Conscious too how English lacks an appropriate
word for that particular region behind the ear.
How 'post-auricular' is surely more painful to say
than walking this dream of un-clocked moments
in the lemon-scented absence of incorrigible felines.

V.

Thus a lady shakes a rug, which may be the essence
of travelogue. Directions and details are necessities,
too, it appears, of the conscious sleepwalker. Let's see.

Left on Antonia López de Bello where a Chilean
flag drapes a satellite dish over a mechanic's shop
and recalls my imagined quest to find Neruda:
to pose the questions to which I'd put
his home and homeland, as the crowds congregate
to enter the sanctums of La Chascona.

Neruda, who encircled the globe in book after book
of questions, wondering: why was it Columbus
failed to discover Spain? And, coincidentally,
how many questions does a cat have?
Or could it really be that for the ants
of the anthill dreams are a duty?

Neruda, whose exhumed bones
were poisoned with nothing more
than poetry.

VI.

But to speak differently in the shade of lemon trees:
in love I arrive, haunted by the news today
of a flight of limitless souls blown out
of existence over the Ukrainian fields.
Primary school kids running screaming
from a playground where death fell from the sky.

Not the earth's end, but a preserved strip of it,
their echoes discord the songs of Santiago's streets.
And, as we walk back past Cruchero Exeter,
low Andean foothill fog makes
of the late afternoon another sunrise.

VII.

I have walked here too long among marvellous birds
and colourful souls, posing questions of travel.
What place does one have? What time does one hold?
What clock does the body drop, fumbling in the wind?
Whose are these hips and angelic dark lashes?
How far *are* we from China? And is that man,
that woman, laughing and singing in the streets,
another tourist, local or business traveller,
each cutting loose the appointed hours?

VIII.

Questions are the answers to unborn questions.
Have the stray dogs mastered the art of graffiti?
Will the airport recognise us when we return?
Does the fighter pilot's conical sonic boom
leave us time to assemble one answer or two?
And though the conscious somnambulist stumbles
on the alternating edges of maps and street corners,
wouldn't it have been a pity not to see this?

But could it be possible (*really* possible) to be
in Curicó or Colchagua, Maipo or Aconcagua?
The itinerary says so. The map is on the phone.
The stray dogs are laughing and everyone else
seems to have gone home. Tomorrow, we'll see.

Mutton Fat Jade

I.

Deep-quarried in the mountains of Kunlun,
chunked, chipped, polished, then polished again.

Seed nephrite sown in the mind of its artificer
as one cream-toned stone like raw mutton fat.

II.

Uygur men and women turn spits of roast lamb
or coax chump-chop cubes on to sticks of *kaorou*.
Sweet lipids drip from the polisher's hands.

III.

Hundreds of miles east, display-cases station
dynasties. I touch the glass and, in my palm,
seem to hold the shape of a hand in jade.

This pair of quail, palm-proportioned, more quail
by nephrite than the taxidermist's dream,
are hands too, yet birds, cuppable, to hold again.

IV.

Outside the leaves of the ginkgo are scallop-shell
sorrel, each leaf a scallop to seed, off-white,

almost the cream of mutton fat but juicier
like leaf-sap or ripest mangostene.

The museum's chill colours the afternoon sun,
its jade a texture, of the tongue.

Leaving Shanghai

This crystal morning
crossing the Huang Pu,

the unfathomable architecture
of last night's multi-coloured

rainbows of light can now
at last be seen.

Leaving Pudong's construction sites,
the batteries of articulated trucks:

upon which digger after digger
unpacked, pristine, with that

unmistakeable gleam of the not-yet-
broken in, sits and is silent.

Their unmatched caterpillar tracks,
like sharpened claws, will clutch

the earth of expo sites, hotels and bars.
And leaves behind, along elevated

arterial roads, the Shanghai girls slimmer
than cirrus and the boys slimmer still.

I saw a man so coiffeured
the suspended dust curtseyed

to his catwalked path, as if he lived
in a world where nothing in particular

falls: the billboards, the LCD screens,
the light redacting channels and paths.

For a moment I have had
the convenience of not living

here at all: always happy to arrive
and happy always, it seems, to leave.

And that is Shanghai or a version of it:
the vast concourses of Hongqiao,

the steaming baskets of *xiaolongbao*,
the taxi drivers less vociferously guttural

than their northern brothers—quiet even—
save for this morning's 'master' who,

un-self-consciously, sings, weaving
between unfailingly black Mercedes-Benz.

And that is Shanghai: a city that appears,
as we leave it, like the latest film

of what might have been,
of what might be and what will.

The Empress of Peonies

So Empress Wu Ze Tian
the petals of the peony,

buxom as Tang women,
proscribed...

By the waters of Luoyang
the faceless Buddhas stand.

But the rock, black rock,
carved of a single sculpture,

in which the pattern
of peonies appears,
also stands.

It is a natural formation,
at least they say
formed naturally...

And I have wondered
if poetry now
is the appearance

of peonies—the pretence
of peonies—in a world
of rock, black rock:

knowing it is neither those
nor superstition of locals.

For we must speak more
quietly—and—slowly

in a world of keyboards
and carnage indistinguishable

in the field hospitals
(military and civilian),

speak—softly—for the faceless,
the woman within the Empress
so softly the buxom peony.

The Solitude of Seeing

How solitary it is
on this uniquely

unpolluted morning
to watch and to listen

not quietly but silently…

Their English sounds
strangely in my ears,

as my lark-pitched
Mandarin must in theirs,

observing also the more
universal exaggerated poses,

how the men incline
their chins to look taller,

how the women straighten
their gazes in reflected

elevator chrome: all
falling somewhere between

how we might wish to look
and how we would like

to appear, though such
explanation lives outside

the experience of seeing…

The traffic speeding towards
us across multiple lanes,

a girl smiling out of millions,
until I open the front door

and your beckoning eyes
allow me at last

to see no more.

The Unorthodox Informer

Who disclaimed in disquisition
of the wind the varieties of birds,
their colours and hiding places.

Who explained the bower bird's
every passing aesthetic whim
to every passer-by.

Who distributed shopping
lists to irrelevant authorities
which disposed of them carefully.

Who reckoned with
unacknowledged legislators
in the ponds of their meeting

and found them wanting,
if no less companionable.

Who despised the people
of the brochures and pop-ups
who might be rightly accused.

Who gave everything
to the public buildings
and would have sold his papers

to the state prisons were it not
innocents might devour them.

Who was under his own surveillance,
seeking everywhere a position
from which to report the beetles,

the snails, the fantastic
security voles,
twitchings in the tram-rails.

Who was not averse
to repeated acts (saving confession).
There were tears in those eyes.

The Bamboo Approach

A rock for all ages
blown to dust

among the usual
foundations...

Node upon node
the bamboo grows,

tusk of cellulose,
nimble lignin,

like a voice from the forest
who speaks often

of the truth
in green reflection.

Spring Sale

Five distinct shades of pink
unpackage their scents

nailed to the unstartled
boughs of these Beijing trees.

Today, across the land,
a billion photographs

will tug at the seams
of tablets and phones,

uncurling posts in reel
upon reel like camera film

of old. But endlessly
composed, cropped

and spliced, flowering
chequerboards

in the private gardens
of certain apps.

Last week the silver birches
shed their caterpillared catkins

about the sand-stormed streets
all but unnoticed.

They reminded me
of the leftover women

and forgotten men
who, after certain ages,

still in bloom are snapped
and framed on the mantelpiece

of the once-and-for-all
unespoused.

The unmarried beautiful women
come (and the unforgettable men)

taking snapshots of themselves
(alone) before the first petals fall.

I recall the silver birches'
impetuous release

like a slingshot
against faltering memory.

The real test of a tree
is not this cat-walked

display of stamens and sex,
but how one makes do

when the earth about one
cracks... standing naked

in the winter wind
like so many leftover men,

as the beautiful forgotten
women unforgettably

are likewise still surviving
somehow in the ancient fields.

Memorandum

If earliest memory
would not invent

so: the first time
I raised my hands

above my head
to cradle a steaming bowl

from a kitchen hatch,
if not the first time

I raised my hands
above my head.

But who could remember?
That March in

the earliest of my childhoods
when the sun shone

the whole month long
and made each impossible

day longer by memory
or closer in fact.

When the soil in the garden
smelt of earth

and could be felt
between your toes and hands.

This may be considered
possible, even likelier

than fiction: as of
a mind considerate

that would remember
such things.

And I would like that

in writing.

A Beijing Duck for My Mother

I.

It is your birthday. You
open the bedroom shutters

onto Durham fields of
incontrovertible green.

The sun is shining, today;
though you expect a spot

of English rain: weather
of the period piece passing

intermittent clouds of now.
Rare breed sheep nudge

tufts of grass and cow parsley
where once an old white horse

nodded on her haunches in the dew-
decked light of twenty years ago.

II.

You are seventy-seven.
For forty-four years you

have been a mother and
for thirty-eight, mine.

I sit in Beijing and write as you
reminisce of a Brighton girlhood

evacuated during the Blitz,
young love, Boston, my father

impressively failing to cross
the Charles River in incomparable

New England snow. High-rise hair
of the 60s, low-rise wages, bungalows

and, as you descend the stair, one or more
homes almost like this (built 1851).

III.

I sit in Beijing, as we both sat
last October, having walked

through fumes of roasted chestnuts
to a private room, chrysanthemum tea

wetting our lips, munching lotus root
before the first wood-smoked duck

was ushered to table. And I, as only
a child can master, unachingly

uninformed, welcoming surprise
that duck was a favourite of yours.

So fortunate I have been in you
for whom there were never favourites

and no self unfavoured
but your own self favouring all.

We spoke of radishes, match-sticked
scallion, garlic minced to unlaced aioli

and the salt-sweet tang of *tianmianjiang*,
dipping the crispest, least oily skin

into an earthenware bowl of sugar:
so *not* very English and so sublime.

Wrapping thin slivers of duck in
pancakes thinner still. And, then,

that Beijing touch, *kongxinshaobing*:
sesame-starred 'hollow-heart' buns,

each the size of a palm, into which,
wholeheartedly, we crammed yet more

duck, scallion, julienned pink radish
knowing, then, that this was how

in the shape of our hands we'd formed
the sheer ingredients of a moment.

IV.

So now, from this desk, five thousand miles
hence, the greatest chefs at my beck,

I've arranged for you your very own
Beijing Duck: not sodden-bagged for sale

across a city's termini, but tender, crisp,
transported at a synapse's speed

to warm your heart at the table of
a wet English house this August day.

And, though I am not there,
I am there: helping you to a wine

lain low and dark for a long time,
from whose cork we pull

the celebratory sound of
18th of the 8th '38...

For I have arranged for us
a table in perpetuity where,

whenever we wish, we may feast
on glistening duck meat, where

I shall be seated beside you,
aching to be informed,

as once again you fold and
unfold the story of you my mother.

Out of Season

If there had been spring,
what little winter said
among frosted buds.

And so to summer:
the green leaves in breath,
the gingko terrifying.

So very scented
the city in the filth
of heat and also

more volatile—
chlorinated bubbles
from the fountains rising—

that I have wondered
how we may survive
that happiness

(that we may not)
in the shortest autumn,
the so very scented

and, what is most
terrifying, that we also
said little suggesting less.

An Expatriate Out of Season

What autumn there was
can only measure spring
in downwind memories.

It is a relief to know
there are relations
beyond my touch,

the decisions liquids make,
as in this: the efflorescence
of cream in your coffee cup

and fluid mechanics
in densities we are told,
having decided nothing.

That country is another,
this a frontier
traversing all others…

Only there is song
in the metaphors of
that darkness—

whosoever may find
a source of relief
in downwind memory…

A song sung
in a seasonal measure
which was not much.

Days Like This

Or when the sky is blue
and the wind blows

the polluted air
beyond the hills,

if not the demented cars
chugging...

To sound the temperament
in a style, by diligence

or twitching hazel,
to attain clarity among

phlegm and characters...

The small, endearing dogs
plump with their owners' loves,

swallows dropping from
pines in mosquito flight,

the unpersuaded discovering
in time an incisive song:

all these, on days like this,
withhold that which

they are given little by little,
which is the greater gift

being themselves
in the blue air being.

GPS

In lieu of appearance,
or a choice of appearances,

the in-flight screen glowing
Pacific to your Atlantic

or driving in the Napa hills…

Are these choices or
prescriptions?

The sloping Silverado Trail,
its noted gradients,

or crossing the valley floor
by cordon-trained vines

oriented to the afternoon sun,
respondent to the moon,

upon the old Niebaum road.
Niebaum, who mapped

the coast of Alaska
and came to rest here:

once Inglenook, then Rubicon,
to Inglenook restored

among the golden contours.

Willows of the Fourth Ring

The willows in the winter wind,
green-yellow octopi or
as the tails of cartoon comets:

such is their movement
without the labourers
who with long poles

coax the last recalcitrant
tawny leaves from branches
which sag without despair.

That was
earlier.

I speak now of a rising nation
resurgent,
of the contested ground

searching not
for the first time
without its borders.

Is it by a revolution of
tentacles or that
spectacular night-lit trail

they will arrive
or are arriving?

There are no sentries
upon the walls,
only tourists biking

atop the enclosed bricks
of Xian and the
Great Wall spreads

its webbed and callused
feet upon the world...

So in winter the willows
blow back upon themselves
and over

the Fourth Ring Road
flying above SUVs that are
death and may be still death.

Surely they are
not honourable.

I will move as the willows move
rooted here, the green and yellow
octopi if not the comet's trailing

and may likewise arrive

and appear spectacular.

Of Anxiety

Having feared or forgot
our most basic tenders,

the checking account
or diastolic charging,

reagents from whose
flare the afternoon turns

upon whose face nothing
remains but the immobile,

we have mislaid
the uses of anxiety:

momentum and motion
toward the intimate

tenders and how we
found them or put each

to good use, yes, worrying
on their accounts,

as if they too might
one day be unmoving,

having feared or forgot
that, whatever the afternoon

light, whether it is or is
not flaring, whether it is

or is not worth facing,
this is a poem's end.

Planes of Honour

'It has been more than ten years since my demotion from the imperial prefecture. During this long lull in activity, I have devoted myself to poetry and have accumulated over a thousand poems. Some are allegorical descriptions of objects, valuable only to the blind [...] Others, composed at intervals with the help of wine, are short and trivial. It was my hope to embody in my poems profound meaning in simple language, to invent new rhymes and rhythms, to create flawless parallelism without sacrificing sense and feeling. However, I fear I have not been able to attain this goal.'

—Yuan Zhen to the Secretariat-Chancellery, Ling Huchu.

I.

The poem lies on the high official's desk.
The poem lies on the high poet's desk.
Each plane shares the hairs of the calligrapher's hand.
Each hand shares the plane of the calligrapher's hairs.

And yet, Yuan Zhen, the poem weighs differently
in your hand, feels almost outside, mouths eternally.
And yet, Ling Huchu, the outside weighs differently
in your hand, feels almost inside, mouths poetically.

II.

These cruder planes fall silent in the frustrated night.
Come morning, or ten years on, we may stroke, line
upon line, from the wood pigeon's dew-sore cooing

to the late bamboo swaying and say: 'Enough.
The wine is good, the air is bright, my light casts
no imperial tint and yet illuminates the page

of each slumberous official who forgets that bed
is bed and be buried in it. Let the flags blaze
with emblems of bears, tigers and unicorns'.

By then and only then, by a thousand songs
and a thousand scrolls. By one scroll and only then,
the high poem, my father, sounds.

In Praise of Saliva

That introduces babe
and mother in whose milk

and the secretive glands
each tooth becomes

acquainted with the cultured
atmosphere of the oral.

That gives us pause
before the first words,

clearing the throat by
upwards of a pint a day.

That nourishes kissing
in the intimate fluid

of being young and
becoming young (again):

a way of being involved
in the tissue cultures.

That precipitates taut
chains of tannin in the

spittoons of every red
sloshed from memory,

as Pavlov's dogs recall
drooling clichés of sound…

And your imploring hips
and the capsaicin of chillies

no less fragrant than
the sea in the mouth rising

as you dribble on your pillow
gently and have me once more

salivating in the dark
for your belonging presence.

Apparition on Broadway

Unusually alone,
traipsing the length
of Broadway

in early middle age,
my airline-scuffed shoes...

Grateful for this
curiously diagonal
Manhattan street in which

I now pace middle ground.

No dark meandering
wood as Dante trod,
no Virgil at the end

of the block anticipating
circles and the certain future.

Until you came to me
and I saw in your eyes
again I was twenty-five

falling in love (at last)
with the rightest woman.

A figure of youth picking
at fries, teaching me (again)
the art of friendship,

conciliation, diagonal affection;
that, as you paced off
in snow boots among

the shadows of a New York
winter, roused my hibernating mind
from the self-induced slumber

of cliché and the sideways glances
of older men all arms akimbo:
knowing you no apparition

but a kind of conscience
of youth crossing the street
until you reached the other side.

Liminal

Sands of the beaches
and of the coastal towns,

brine of the melancholy
air, salinity that baulks

not at the ocean but lives
in enveloping waves

which yet may
(not) freeze...

Considering those lost
in the small communities

they say *to the sea*
and in the rest-homes

and hospices in which
no peace but peace is made.

The sea therapeutic?
But you saying:

is it because we are
water also?

At *The Captain's Arms*
the old dog thinks not,

licking his wounds
as the fretful moss

that survives (like him)
upon fear's nutrition.

So the dismembered masters
who likewise believe in fate:

as one is walking
roaring to the water's edge

insisting he return
from whence he came.

My Last Rites

There will be a cremation,
which is at least considerate,

unless by some miracle
my organs merit donation.

The music, Stravinsky's
Symphony of Psalms III,

the *laudate*, sung by
Westminster Cathedral Choir

or, if they are unavailable,
the James O'Donnell

recording will do.
And ten or maybe fifteen

cats wandering freely
for those of a feline

affinity who may stroke
them in their laps.

At the wake, all
manner of pickled foods

and marinated garlic
all may smell

and seventeen back vintages
of choicest Australian Shiraz

which once were said
to have made

Peter Reading
snort with joy,

alongside a punch
of mango and freshest

mangostene (for those
who joy without).

No priest or functionary,
not even a Buddhist

at the back, unless
he understands

the language of cats.
No poetry either

(not a word of poetry):
apart from one poem

in the programme
for those who do not

love Stravinsky
and one for those who do.

A Dawning

Some revelations grow
from the ground,

some from the
burning hearth,

some from
the inquisitive mind

sketching possibility
in the sand.

Still others come
from another,

untrammelled, unaneled
who looks over the edge

of morning and adorns
nothing in the circumference

of our lives but the darkness
of the unsetting sun.

Terminal

A moth wizened
upon its back, dead

I had assumed, sprang
momentarily to life

and crossed the paved
Australian kitchen floor

in drunken spirals,
one leg decimated

by some vexed
narrative of flight.

Illuminations of Beijing

I.

The first light is the dullest light:
reflecting the uncertain brightness

of a winter's day. The first light
reveals buildings and trees

and the cracked earth
of winter fields.

The first light is suggestion,
conception, then realisation

or so it seems. For I can
never say precisely where

this city begins:
only that it ends

in these gently illuminated
calcareous hills.

II.

There is no returning
to that first light.

Not even in the imagined
rays of another day.

Tomorrow not yet visible
in the early morning light,

in the early morning light
scarcely an idea, though it must

resemble what one sees here:
solitary figures in the trees

practising *taiji*, calligraphers
shedding meaning in gleam

upon gleam of water strokes
evaporating all too swiftly

from the winding paths
of parks and palaces.

Nor at mid-morning may one
speak of a second or third light.

For the gradual day rises
in this arc of the sun

accompanying everyone,
almost unnoticed now

at midday in which the tower
blocks stand in the height

of their clarity. From which
the people come hungry,

boisterous, expectant
in the azure-coloured sun.

III.

Winter. Condensation at the glass.
Joy of steam at hot-pot or the

evaporating warmth of noodle
bowls nursing nostrils and slurps.

Vendors of caramel-encrusted
crabapple and roasted chestnuts

cry their wares. Lunchtime light
refracted in twisted screens

of caramel glaze, molar-encoating,
engorgingly tart, shining through

charcoal smoke and the condensing
breaths of every one of us:

each adding one more day
to the laden shelves of experience.

IV.

Jungle birds whirling in the noise
of fan-belts chugging slowly on.

Fur-encircled faces of the beautiful
girls and the less beautiful

beautiful in their fur-encircled worlds:
wild foxes in the snow

surviving from day to day
in the frozen streets.

And the boys smoking like men
in their hearts imagining men.

We have none of us not felt
the inscription of these marks

and the light they bring
as the last autumn leaves

skitter and scratch their pathetic
ways along dry sidewalks

and the cracked pavements
of the canals in which

no foxes play, but where
the smart new dogs

frolic in the encircling arms
of their owners' loves.

V.

This heart that pumps
and is replaced by the replacing

blood for the most part
outside of light…

Were each part, each molecule
to correspond with each

new feeling, then our loves
and our hearts would be one.

Instead, we skitter and scratch
in the winter sun, tirelessly

accommodating this thought
and that arm, imagining

the wild foxes, the yappety dogs
and people as they really are.

Sometimes calibrating,
as in the actor's brightest roles

or the clarity of a love
finally expressed in body

and voice and in the sounds
between all spoken words

that in between their breaths
keep on illuminating the world.

VI.

Now a softer afternoon light
offsets the shadows of buildings

in stark relief, orange contours
of metal and brick. Amazing

how the gingko still maintains
its orangeade leaves even now.

These shadows behind us
that are not our pasts,

nor even the futures
of those afternoons

where once more we hope
our shadows remain behind,

as if today appeared nothing
more than a walk to work

taken in reverse,
these shadows

are the same…

Here, as you walk from east
to west, the sun setting

so very slowly it seems,
with all the eastern names

of the city arriving in all
the western names of this city,

the significance of these shadows
threatens subtlety and cannot escape.

VII.

The last light and the first light
the same; or cousins

at the end of day. The last light…
its absence almost sudden,

though such departure implied
all along the sense of an ending.

A controlled dimming of the house
in the theatre of the world.

This is the last light
and this is the last moment

of this day, as precisely
it appears in the closing

of its hours as in every way
its own unique stare

and in every way also
the same. And I feel, now,

this is the last time,
impatient of epiphany,

I may see the world
and these calcareous hills,

softening caramel-crusted crabapple
in the back of our mouths.

Hoping we may somehow
return or at least perhaps

make it home; and will
venture once more outside

in the brilliant light
forever failing.

Fragment: After Sappho

] heart
] absolutely
] I can

holding unfailing
or as the cartographer
Jia Dan wrote:

To narrow down
the world upon
a piece of silk.

Sappho [   ] for us
now centuries
left wondering

who the woman with violets
in her lap could be
[   ]

And would she weep now
for what Egypt saved
in the tatters and [   ]

of papyrus? Or wouldn't
her tears fall rather
for the violet woman

] and her desire
between silk sheets
] the clouds passing

if not winter
] and she [   ]
holding unfailing?

] heart
] absolutely
] I can

Notes

Occasional Chinese words in these poems have been rendered in 'pinyin': the alphabetical transcription of Mandarin Chinese. As the pronunciation of 'pinyin' can be counter-intuitive for English speakers, some of the below notes suggest approximate pronunciations as a guide to how the poems sound.

Epigraph: from *If Not, Winter: Fragments of Sappho* trans. Anne Carson (New York: Alfred A. Knopf, 2002).

Holding Unfailing: 'there were a world / elsewhere', in Shakespeare's *Coriolanus*, Coriolanus, on his banishment, defiantly affirms 'There is a world elsewhere' (Act 3, Scene 3).

Great Southern in Crystal: 'elephant-hind rocks' refers to Elephant Rocks, near the coastal town of Denmark, Western Australia. These weathered formations resemble the bodies of elephants.

Path Finding: Mount Barker and Margaret River, two important wine regions in Western Australia.

Wang Ao and the Lobster: Wang Ao 王敖 (b. 1976) is a leading Chinese poet, some of whose work and research relates to Classical Chinese poetry. He has published five collections of poetry and was the recipient of the *Anne Kao Poetry Prize*. As a translator, he has translated into Mandarin Chinese such poets as Seamus Heaney, W. H. Auden, Hart Crane and Wallace Stevens. He is Assistant Professor of Asian Languages and Literatures at Wesleyan University.

Guang Hua Road: 'Guang Hua Lu' 光华路 or Guang Hua Road is a major Beijing thoroughfare in the city's CBD. '[T]he CCTV tower's / cross-hatched rubik's gleam': to the north-east of Guang Hua bridge lies the site of China Central Television (CCTV)'s Headquarters designed by Rem Koolhaas and Ole Sheeren. 'Guo Mao': to the south-west is Guo Mao 国贸, a.k.a the China World complex, made up of a convention centre, hotels, offices and, at the time of writing, numerous construction sites.

The Human Chain: *'A man who used to notice such things'* is from Thomas Hardy's 'Afterwards'. 'Yeats's gaffer': refers to the gaffer in W. B. Yeats's 'Broken Dreams'. 'Glanced through Kavanagh's / hedgerows or the slats of an innocent fence': see Patrick Kavanagh's 'Innocence'. 'Eliot's city for you yet more unreal': the 'Unreal city' of T. S. Eliot's *The Waste Land*. '[A]s MacNeice would warn, the bridges down or unusable: / the only option Charon's ferry / *faute de mieux*, obols jangling / in his black hands': see Louis MacNeice's 'Charon'.

Untitled: William Shakespeare (1564-1616), William Wordsworth (1770-1850), Wallace Stevens (1879-1955), George Oppen (1908-1984). *'Mr Wordsworth is not accustomed to being / interrupted...'*: a variation on Cowden Clarke's recollection of Keats's dinner with the Wordsworths in January 1817.

Arrival at Santiago: see Elizabeth Bishop's 'Arrival at Santos' and 'Questions of Travel' and Pablo Neruda's *The Book of Questions*. 'Don Melchor's foundation': Don Melchor de Santiago Concha y Toro (1833-1892) planted vines in the Maipo Valley in the 1880s and was the original founder of the wine producing company which bears his name. 'La Chascona': Pablo Neruda's Santiago home.

Mutton Fat Jade: *'kaorou'* 烤肉 pronounced 'cow row' ('row' as in 'row of streets') is literally roasted meat, usually roast mutton on sticks, popular in Xinjiang cuisine and commonly eaten also in Beijing.

Leaving Shanghai: 'Hongqiao' 虹桥 pronounced 'hong chow' is the site of one of Shanghai's major railway stations and an international airport; *'xiaolongbao'* 小笼包 pronounced 'show' (as in the 'show' of 'shower'), 'long', 'bow' (as in a 'ship's bow') are soup-filled dumplings, a Shanghai speciality.

The Empress of Peonies: 'Wu Ze Tian' 武則天 (624-705 C.E.) reportedly banished the peony flower during her remarkable reign of China (690-705 C.E). The flower survived in 'Luoyang' 洛阳—pronounced 'law-yang'—the city in Henan Province where the Longmen Buddhist statues are found. There is a black rock structure at the Longmen gorge whose patterning resembles peonies.

A Beijing Duck for My Mother: *'tianmianjiang'* 甜面酱 is a salty, sweet sauce made from fermented flour and soy which accompanies Beijing Duck. Some Beijing Duck restaurants also offer *'kongxinshaobing'* 空心烧饼 (pronounced, roughly, 'kong-shin-show-bing', as in the 'show' of 'shower'), thin sesame buns with 'empty hearts' intended to be filled with duck.

GPS: 'Niebaum', Gustave Niebaum (1842-1908) was the original founder of the Inglenook winery in California's Napa Valley, now owned and fully restored by Francis Ford Coppola.

Planes of Honour: 'Yuan Zhen' 元稹 (779-831 C.E.), a major Chinese poet of the Tang Dynasty.

Fragment: After Sappho: 'Jia Dan' 贾耽 (730-805 C.E.), Tang Dynasty Chinese official and cartographer.